Fossil
Seekers

By Laura Buller

CELEBRATION PRESS
Pearson Learning Group

The following people from **Pearson Learning Group**
have contributed to the development of this product:

Joan Mazzeo, Jennifer Visco **Design** | **Editorial** Betsy Niles, Linette Mathewson
Christine Fleming **Marketing** | **Publishing Operations** Jennifer Van Der Heide
Production Laura Benford-Sullivan
Content Area Consultants Dr. Amy Rabb Liu and Dr. Charles Liu

The following people from **DK** have
contributed to the development of this product:

Art Director Rachael Foster

Nick Avery, Ann Cannings **Design** | **Managing Editor** Scarlett O'Hara
Cynthia Frazer, Helen McFarland **Picture Research** | **Editorial** Steve Setford, Kate Pearce
Richard Czapnik, Andy Smith **Cover Design** | **Production** Rosalind Holmes
David Lambert **Consultant** | **DTP** David McDonald

Dorling Kindersley would like to thank: Carole Oliver for additional design work, Jo Dixon for border artworks, and
Johnny Pau for additional cover design work.

Picture Credits: American Museum Of Natural History: 14tl, 17t, 18b, 18t, 19t. Ardea London Ltd: © D.Parer & E.Parer Cook 5br. Art Directors &
TRIP: M. Lee 10–11b. Associated Press AP: Jalil Bounhar 5t. Carnegie Museum of Natural History, Pittsburgh, PA: 14–15b. Corbis: Annie Griffiths Belt
3; Bettmann 16b, 19br, 20b, 21t; Didier Dutheil 15tl; Derek Hall/Frank Lane Picture Agency 8bl; Layne Kennedy 25t; Richard T. Nowitz 30;
Stapleton Collection 7br. DK Images: 11bl; Jon Hughes 11t. Kobal Collection: Amblin/Universal 28–29b. Museum of the Rockies: 22, 23t, 26b, 27t.
The Natural History Museum, London: 11br. Louie Psihoyos ©psihoyos.com: 28t. University of Queensland: Scott Hucknull 20tr. Science Photo
Library: 6tl, 13br; Sheila Terry 13t. Smithsonian Institution: Credit line: National Museum of Natural History ©2003 Smithsonian Institution 1.
Cover: Corbis: Annie Griffiths Belt front t. Louie Psihoyos ©psihoyos.com: front b.

All other images: ☒ Dorling Kindersley © 2005. For further information see www.dkimages.com

ISBN: 0-7652-5214-7

Color reproduction by Colourscan, Singapore
Printed and bound in China by Leo Paper Products Ltd.
1 2 3 4 5 6 7 8 9 10   08 07 06 05 04

1-800-321-3106
www.pearsonlearning.com

Contents

Discovering Fossils 4

Mary Anning..............................6

Barnum Brown 14

Jack Horner 22

Discoveries Continue 30

Glossary...31

Index 32

Paleontologists uncover the remains of a ten-million-year-old rhinoceros near Orchard, Nebraska.

Discovering Fossils

Imagine leaving the classroom and stepping back in time to the age when dinosaurs walked on Earth. You look around. Many unfamiliar plants surround you. Unusual insects buzz by under a canopy of tall trees. A strange noise startles you. You turn around. Suddenly, you are face to face with a real live dinosaur!

Of course, this could never happen. Dinosaurs are **extinct**. They all died millions of years ago. So how do we know so much about dinosaurs if no one has ever seen one?

The *Giganotosaurus* dinosaur, one of the largest predatory dinosaurs, could grow to 45 feet and weigh almost nine tons.

One way to find out about ancient forms of life is through fossils. Fossils are the remains of once-living things. Bones, teeth, skin, even footprints can be preserved in the layers of the rocks that make up Earth. Scientists who study fossils are called paleontologists (pay-lee-ahn-TAH-luh-jihsts). They have to be smart, curious, and sometimes adventurous—traveling to wild places to find the clues they need. This book is about three paleontologists who have helped bring the past to life.

Paleontologists at Work
Paleontologists on a "dig" in Morocco use hammers, chisels, and brushes to search for clues about life in the past. They must be patient and persistent while digging for fossils. For example, it can take months or even years to collect enough bones to put together a dinosaur skeleton.

Today's largest reptile, the crocodile, can grow to 16 feet and weigh up to one ton.

5

Mary Anning

1799–1847

Birthplace:
Lyme Regis, Dorset,
England

Discovered:
The first plesiosaur fossil

In 1799, Mary Anning was born in Lyme Regis, in Dorset, England. In the 1700s, people found strange things in the ground, but they were often unsure what they were. Some looked like stone snakes. Others looked like teeth or bones made of stone. People dug them up and called them "curiosities." They were really fossils.

Some people used these fossils as medicine or carried them for luck. Others collected them. Not many people tried to learn what they were or where they came from.

Mary first discovered her love of fossil collecting with her father, Richard Anning. When he wasn't working as a carpenter or cabinetmaker, he collected fossils as a way to earn extra money. Mary enjoyed walking the beaches and climbing the nearby cliffs with her father, searching for fossils to sell.

Mary's father taught her to clean the fossils carefully. He showed her how to add to their value by polishing them and displaying them well. Mary learned how to sell fossils with the help of her father.

This 1825 painting shows the view across Lyme Bay toward Lyme Regis. Lyme was a busy fishing port in Mary's time.

Animal to Fossil

1. When an animal dies, layers of sand or mud quickly bury it.

2. Over thousands to millions of years, the layers of mud turn to rock. The animal's skeleton becomes stonelike, as minerals fill spaces or replace the calcium in the bone.

3. Earth's crust shifts. Buried bones slowly move closer to the surface.

Ammonites have coiled shells in which sea creatures once lived.

Ammonites were once in the world's oceans and now appear as fossils in rocks at Lyme Regis and other beaches around the world.

Selling Fossils

Mary's father died when she was eleven years old. The Anning family had no savings and owed money. Mary's older brother, Joseph, was learning a **trade** so he could earn a living. Mary returned to the shore, looking for fossils.

One day, Mary found a "snake-stone." It was the fossil of a sea animal that we now call an ammonite. As Mary was taking it home, a woman asked if she could buy it. The money Mary received for the fossil was enough to buy food for a week. After that, Mary and her brother both kept searching for fossils.

One day, Joseph found what looked like a crocodile's head with huge eyes and lots of teeth. Almost a year later, Mary found the rest of the skeleton. The creature was about 17 feet long. It looked somewhat like a fish with ribs similar to a lizard. Years after Mary's discovery, a scientist named the skeleton *Ichthyosaurus* (IHK-thee-uh-SOHR-uhs). A local fossil collector bought this strange fossil from the Annings. The money he paid helped support Mary and her family for half a year. Still, Mary and her brother struggled to make a living finding and selling fossils. It sometimes took days or weeks to dig out and clean one fossil.

Ichthyosaurus means "fish lizard." This marine reptile swam by moving its tail from side to side.

This is the skull of an ichthyosaur. The ichthyosaur that Mary and her brother discovered prompted scientists to ask questions about ancient life.

Becoming a Fossil Expert

Mary wanted to know more about the fossils she found. One day, she did a favor for a woman in town. The woman gave her a **geology** book in return. Mary began to read everything she could about rocks. She learned which rocks most often held fossils.

This knowledge helped Mary recognize the best places to find fossils. She learned that the layers of clay and limestone in the cliffs near her home had once been part of a tropical sea, millions of years before. The sea water **eroded** the rock on the cliffs and exposed the fossils of ancient sea creatures.

It was along the cliffs of Lyme Regis that Mary Anning discovered her fossils.

10

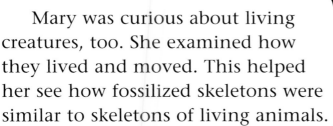

Mary was curious about living creatures, too. She examined how they lived and moved. This helped her see how fossilized skeletons were similar to skeletons of living animals.

Over the years, Mary found more ichthyosaur skeletons. She was the first to discover a complete skeleton of a plesiosaur (PLEE-see-uh-sohr), another type of ocean reptile. She also found the remains of a flying reptile, *Pterodactylus* (tehr-uh-DAK-tih-luhs).

Pterodactylus means "wing finger." The wings of this reptile were flaps of skin attached to long finger bones.

These are the fossilized bones of a plesiosaur's flipper. Plesiosaurs used their huge flippers to paddle through the ocean.

Plesiosaurus, a type of plesiosaur

Mary Becomes Famous

Mary became an expert at putting fossilized skeletons together. People came to know her because of her talent for finding fossils. Scientists were interested in Mary's work, too. Her fossil discoveries were valuable to them.

People began visiting Lyme Regis because of Mary and her fossils. Mary helped these people find fossils. Some visitors were scientists who were trying to understand the history of Earth. Mary learned a lot from these scientists. She borrowed articles they had written and copied them word for word, trying to understand their ideas.

Mary ran a shop in Lyme Regis, where she sold the fossils she had collected.

This picture, painted by Mary's friend, Henry de la Beche, shows how ancient sealife may have looked.

Scientists also learned a lot from Mary, which was unusual for the time. In the early 1800s, women were not taken seriously. Also, most fossil seekers were wealthy people. Still, Mary, a hard-working, self-taught scientist, gained the respect from scientists everywhere. The fossils she found persuaded scientists to think about Earth in new ways.

Mary spent her whole life looking for fossils. Her discoveries helped people picture the plants and animals in ancient seas. Today, many of Mary's fossils are on display in museums around the world.

Gideon Mantell was another fossil hunter in the 1800s. He visited Mary at her shop in Lyme Regis.

Barnum Brown

1873–1963

 Birthplace:
Kansas,
United States

 Discovered:
The first fossil of the
dinosaur *Tyrannosaurus rex*

Barnum Brown loved fossils and began collecting them at a young age. Born in Kansas in 1873, he grew up to be one of the greatest fossil collectors. Unlike Mary Anning, who found fossils below the cliffs in England, Barnum discovered his first fossils in the fields of Kansas. He followed a farmer's plow and collected fossilized seashells **unearthed** by the plow's blades.

In 1892, Barnum began college at the University of Kansas. He was always fascinated by paleontology, even though he studied the arts and engineering. Barnum loved collecting fossils more than attending his college classes.

Before graduating many years later, Barnum went to work at the American Museum of Natural History in New York City. The director of the museum believed a dinosaur collection would attract more visitors to the museum. He sent Barnum to look for dinosaur fossils.

Barnum traveled out West to Wyoming in 1897. He visited a place with so many dinosaur bones that a sheep rancher had built a cabin out of them. While there, Barnum discovered an *Apatosaurus* (uh-pat-uh-SOHR-uhs) skeleton. This huge, plant-eating dinosaur once weighed more than 20 tons and measured 70 feet long.

Dinosaur Inspiration
In 1997, paleontologist Paul Sereno examined the claw of a newly discovered dinosaur in the Sahara Desert. Paul first became interested in dinosaurs in the late 1970s when he visited the American Museum of Natural History. His tour of the dinosaur collection inspired him to study paleontology.

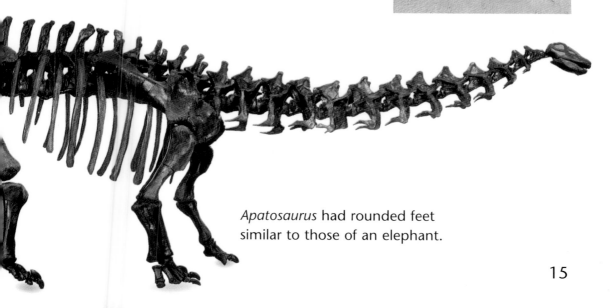

Apatosaurus had rounded feet similar to those of an elephant.

Traveling Fossil Seeker

After three years of fossil hunting, Barnum returned to New York City. His discoveries were taken to the American Museum of Natural History and put on display. Just after Barnum's return, the museum director asked him to search for more fossils—this time in South America. The ship on which he was to travel to Argentina was leaving in three hours. Barnum wrote in his journal, "Imagine getting an outfit [a group of people] together in three hours to go on a 7,000-mile journey, and be gone for a year or more. Such is the life of a fossil man." Barnum accepted the job and made it to the ship on time.

This picture shows Barnum Brown (on left) discussing a *Triceratops* skeleton with another scientist.

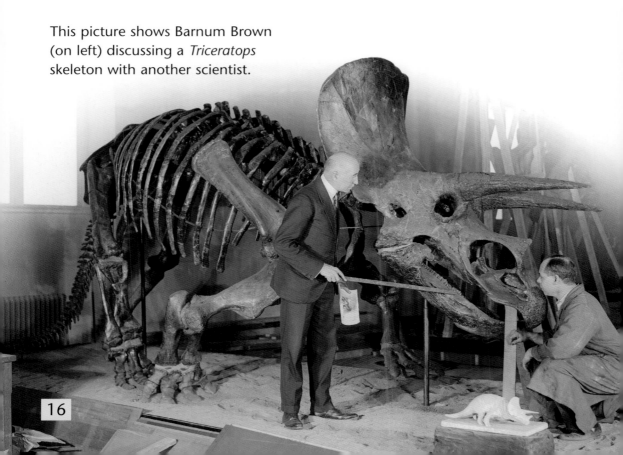

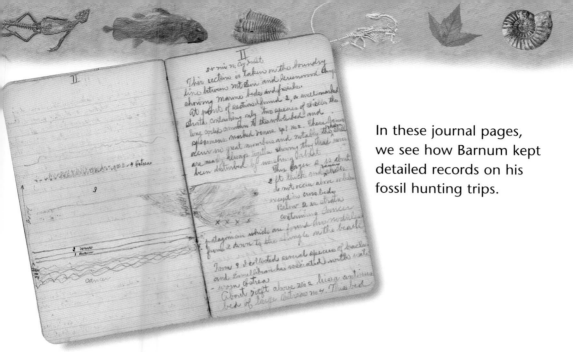

In these journal pages, we see how Barnum kept detailed records on his fossil hunting trips.

Barnum spent more than a year in South America but didn't uncover any major fossils. When Barnum returned to the United States, his friend showed him a fossil and asked if he could **identify** it. Barnum recognized the fossil as part of the horn of a *Triceratops* (try-SEHR-uh-tahps). He was always ready for another hunt. He decided to explore eastern Montana, the area where the *Triceratops* fossil had been found.

While in Montana, Barnum found many fossils, including a *Triceratops* skull and duckbill dinosaur skeletons. He also found the buried skeleton of a huge animal. Using pickaxes, shovels, and chisels, Barnum and his crew dug out the fossils. It took them several months to collect all the animal's remains.

Triceratops, meaning "three-horned face," used its horns and bony neck-frill to defend itself against its enemies.

Once the carnivore fossils had been excavated, they were placed in wooden crates to be transported to the museum.

Finally, all the fossils were packed and carried by train to the American Museum of Natural History. Barnum had discovered the remains of a large **carnivore** with long, sharp teeth. The director of the museum named this dinosaur *Tyrannosaurus rex* (tuh-RAN-uh-sohr-uhs-REKS), or "tyrant lizard king." Barnum was the first to discover *Tyrannosaurus rex*.

While other museum staff mounted and displayed the newly discovered dinosaur, Barnum searched for more bones. In 1908, he found another *T. rex* skeleton, this time with a complete skull. Barnum called it "my favorite child."

Barnum (on right) worked with other scientists to carefully put the fossils back together.

In 1910, Barnum heard about a new area to explore in Canada. Along the Red Deer River in Alberta, hillsides had been eroded and fossils exposed. Barnum and his crew took many trips down this river on a raft. They searched miles and miles of land. Barnum found many tons of bones there, some belonging to dinosaurs never before discovered. Again, he shipped all his finds back to the museum.

In the 1920s, Barnum traveled to countries around the world—including Mexico and India. He continued uncovering fossils. Barnum's wife, Lilian, went with him on many of his explorations. She wrote three books detailing their work and adventures.

This group of fossil seekers wore veils for protection against insects on the Red Deer River.

Lilian Brown often went fossil hunting with Barnum. They found these dinosaur bones in Howe Quarry, Wyoming, in 1941.

19

Barnum's Fossil Collection

In the 1930s, Barnum returned to Montana and Wyoming. There, he and his crew found a huge number of dinosaur fossils. Most of these were the remains of sauropods (SOHR-uh-pahdz), with long necks and huge bodies. It was as if a whole herd of these dinosaurs had died at once.

Barnum wondered how these sauropods had lived and died. Scientists now believe that the sauropods died because of a drought. The lakes and streams the dinosaurs drank from probably dried up, and the sauropods could no longer survive.

A Dinosaur Named Elliot

Australia's largest dinosaur, a sauropod nicknamed Elliot, was found in Queensland, in 2001. Paleontologist Dr. Steve Salisbury (shown above) of the Queensland Museum was part of the team that discovered Elliot.

Barnum found these fossils in Wyoming, in 1934. The bones were numbered so that the skeleton could be reassembled back at the museum.

Barnum spent thirty-five years working for the American Museum of Natural History.

Barnum Brown continued working for the American Museum of Natural History until 1942. Even after that, he guided visitors through the fossil exhibits. He showed off his collection until his death at the age of eighty-nine.

When Barnum started working at the museum, there wasn't one dinosaur there. Barnum and other fossil seekers worked hard to collect and assemble the dinosaur fossils. Now the American Museum of Natural History has the largest dinosaur collection in the world.

This is the specimen found by Brown in 1908. It was the first *Tyrannosaurus* skeleton ever built.

Jack Horner

1943–

Birthplace:
Shelby, Montana,
United States

Discovered:
Fossilized dinosaur nests and
baby duckbill dinosaurs

Jack Horner always loved to discover things. When he was a boy in Shelby, Montana, he spent time exploring the outdoors and searching for treasures. He often found them, too. Jack still has the first fossil he ever collected.

School was difficult for Jack, but he loved learning and always did well in science. After leaving school, he went to the University of Montana. He took every geology and paleontology course he could, but he never completed his degree. Instead, Jack took a position working with fossils at the Princeton Museum of Natural History in New Jersey.

At the museum, Jack was surrounded by other people's fossil finds. He cleaned and organized them. Every summer, however, Jack returned to Montana, where he could dig for fossils himself.

It wasn't enough for Jack to collect dinosaur fossils. He wanted to know everything about dinosaurs. He wanted to know what they looked like and how they lived. Jack was especially interested in duckbill dinosaurs. He wanted to find bones from baby duckbills, but he didn't know where to look.

In the laboratory of the Museum of the Rockies, Jack holds the skull of a *Hypacrosaurus* (hy-PAK-roh-SOHR-uhs) dinosaur.

Duckbill dinosaurs, like this *Corythosaurus* (kuh-RIHTH-uh-SOHR-uhs), had broad beaks for stripping leaves from plants.

Jack Horner named the dinosaur that made this nest *Maiasaura* (my-uh-SOHR-uh), which means "good mother lizard."

Discovering "Egg Mountain"

In 1978, Jack visited a rock shop in Bynum, Montana. The owner had a coffee can full of fossils and asked Jack to identify them. "What I had in my hand," Jack said later, "was a bone from a baby dinosaur, a duckbill—exactly what I wanted, in a place I never expected to find it." The owner of the rock shop told Jack where she had found the fossils. He finally knew where to dig.

Jack and a friend started searching an area that they later named Egg Mountain. They didn't just find baby duckbill fossils. They found whole nests with fossilized babies and eggs in them.

This amazing discovery gave Jack a new understanding of how dinosaurs might have lived. Duckbills didn't act like lizards, as everyone believed. Lizards laid eggs and left them to hatch, but duckbills seemed to care about their hatchlings. The duckbill's behavior was more bird-like than lizard-like. Jack's fossil discoveries were put on display at the museum in Princeton. They made people question the belief that dinosaurs had similar behaviors to lizards.

Fossil Collections
All the fossils in a museum's collection are organized by paleontologists. First, the fossils are cleaned. Then the paleontologists gather and record important information about each fossil.

Unlike most modern reptiles, *Maiasaura* seems to have cared for its young after they hatched from their eggs.

Questions and Answers

In 1982, Jack left his job in New Jersey and went to work at the Museum of the Rockies in Montana. He studied and taught at the museum in the winter months but continued to dig for fossils each summer. His findings were put on display at the museum in Montana.

He continued to ask questions. How did dinosaurs live? What did they eat? Were they warm-blooded? He wanted to learn how they changed as they grew. He was also curious about their behavior. Did they live in herds? Did they **migrate**? Did they all take care of their young?

Fighting Dinosaurs
Zofia Kielan-Jaworowska, a Polish paleontologist, uncovered dinosaur fossils in Mongolia in 1971. The position in which two of the dinosaur fossils were found suggested they died fighting each other.

Jack's fossil discoveries have led him to come up with new ideas about how dinosaurs lived.

In 2003, Jack found his eighth *T. rex* in the rocks in Montana.

To answer questions like these, Jack tried to find as many skeletons of one kind, or **species**, of dinosaur as possible. Then he compared the bones of each skeleton to learn how dinosaurs grew. He also examined the plant and animal fossils in different layers of rocks. This helped him learn about the **habitats** in which dinosaurs lived.

Jack studied exactly how the fossils lay when they were discovered. This helped him learn how dinosaurs behaved. He also tried to understand how and why dinosaurs changed over the millions of years they roamed Earth.

Paleontologists make maps of fossil finds. Sometimes the location of a fossil can tell them about the animal's habitat or how it died.

New Ideas About *T. rex*

In 1990, almost 90 years after Barnum's *Tyrannosaurus rex* discoveries in Montana, Jack and his crew dug up another *T. rex*. For the next few years, they cleaned the bones. Then in 2000, Jack and his crew found five more *T. rex* skeletons. One *T. rex* measured more than 40 feet long. Like Barnum, Jack studied the *T. rex* bones to learn more about this dinosaur's behavior and habits.

As scientists like Jack Horner find more *T. rex* skeletons, they can learn how these fierce-looking dinosaurs really lived.

One question Jack is exploring is how *T. rex* obtained food. Most paleontologists think *T. rex* was a **predator**, hunting down and killing animals to eat. Jack has a different idea—he thinks *T. rex* might have been a **scavenger** instead. He believes it ate the flesh of animals already dead. Maybe it both scavenged and hunted.

Jack keeps searching for more information that will prove his ideas right or wrong. He continues to dig up fossils. He continues to ask questions and search for answers about how dinosaurs lived.

Jack Horner worked on the *Jurassic Park* movies, helping to make sure the dinosaurs in the films were as realistic as possible.

Discoveries Continue

Paleontologists share their discoveries, check each other's work, and sometimes come to different conclusions. Some of them want to know what ancient creatures looked like. Others are more interested in finding out how ancient creatures behaved. Still others want to learn how living things have changed over time. Together, these fossil seekers are continuing to bring the past to life.

These fossil hunters are digging for dinosaur remains at Egg Mountain in Montana.

Glossary

carnivore	a meat-eating animal
eroded	worn away by wind or water
extinct	no longer alive or existing
geology	the science that studies Earth's rocks and soil
habitats	types of places where plants or animals live
identify	to show someone or something to be a certain person or thing
migrate	to move from one place to another in search of food or better living conditions
predator	an animal that captures and eats other animals
scavenger	an animal that eats dead and decaying flesh
species	a particular kind of living thing
trade	skilled work done with the hands to earn money
unearthed	dug up from the earth

Index

Alberta, Canada 19
American Museum of Natural
    History 15, 16, 18, 21
ammonite 8
Anning, Joseph 8, 9
Anning, Mary 6–13
Anning, Richard 7, 8
Apatosaurus 15
Argentina 16
Brown, Barnum 14–21, 28
Brown, Lillian 19
Corythosaurus 23
De la Beche, Henry 13
duckbill dinosaur 17, 22, 23,
    24, 25
Egg Mountain 24, 30
Horner, Jack 22–29
Hypacrosaurus 23
ichthyosaur 9
India 19
Jurassic Park 29
Kansas 14
Kielan-Jaworowska, Zofia 26
Lyme Regis, England
    6, 7, 8, 10, 12, 13
Maiasaura 24, 25
Mantell, Gideon 13

Mexico 19
Mongolia 26
Montana 17, 20, 22, 23, 24,
    26, 27, 28, 30
Museum of the Rockies 23, 26
plesiosaur 6, 11
Plesiosaurus 11
predator 29
Pterodactylus 11
Queensland, Australia 20
Red Deer River 19
Sahara Desert 15
Salisbury, Steve Dr. 20
sauropods 20
scavenger 29
Sereno, Paul 15
T. rex (see also *Tyrannosaurus
    rex*) 18, 27, 28, 29
Triceratops 16, 17
Tyrannosaurus rex 14, 18, 21, 28
Wyoming 15, 19, 20